Tink Tink

Retold by Becca Heddle
Illustrated by Isobel Lundie

OXFORD
UNIVERSITY PRESS

They zoom up into the air.

Tink Tink pops up.

Owl tells Tink Tink to hop into a pit.

Owl waits and waits.
He is cross with Tink Tink.

Owl naps.
Now Tink Tink is off.

Retell the story

Once upon a time ...

The end